Impressum
Verlag: BABADADA GmbH, Nedderfeld 112 , 22529 Hamburg
Geschäftsführer / Verlagsleitung: Harald Hof
Druck: Books on Demand GmbH, In de Tarpen 42, 22848 Norderstedt

Imprint
Publisher: BABADADA GmbH, Nedderfeld 112 , 22529 Hamburg, Germany
Managing Director / Publishing direction: Harald Hof
Print: Books on Demand GmbH, In de Tarpen 42, 22848 Norderstedt

school

lekol

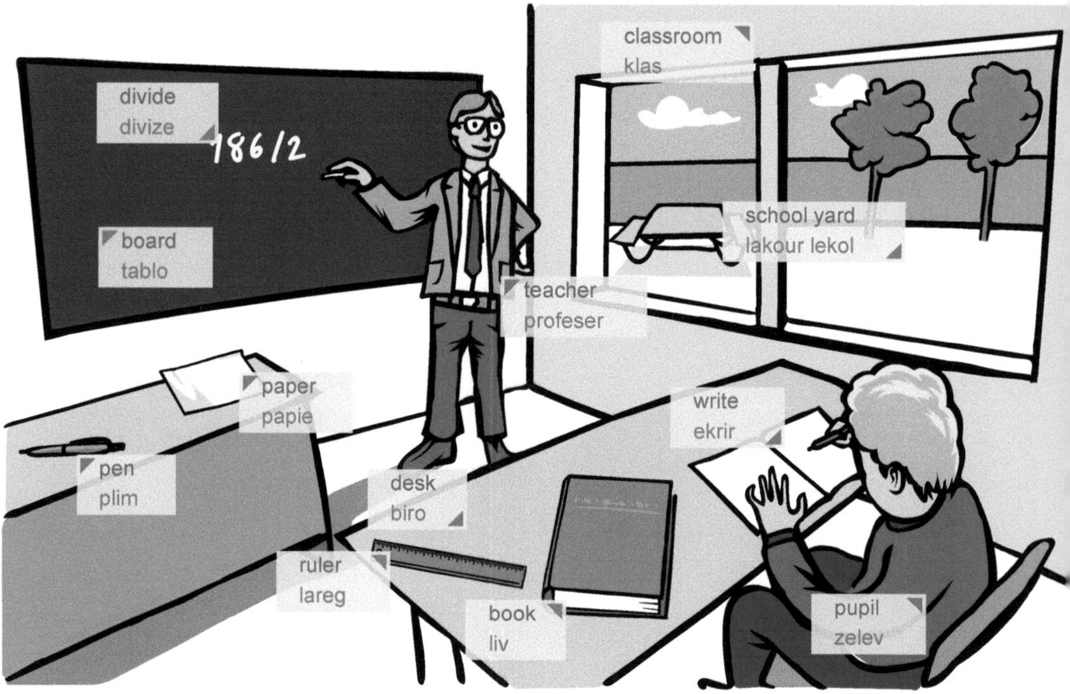

classroom
klas
divide
divize
186/2
board
tablo
school yard
lakour lekol
teacher
profeser
paper
papie
write
ekrir
pen
plim
desk
biro
ruler
lareg
book
liv
pupil
zelev

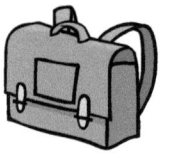

satchel

sak lekol

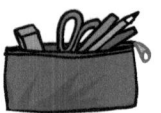

pencil case

plimie

pencil

kreyon

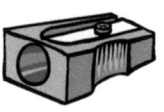

pencil sharpener

egizwar

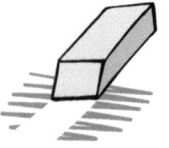

rubber

gom

drawing pad

kaye desin

drawing

desin

paintbrush

pinso

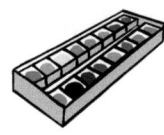

paint box

bwat lapintir

scissors

sizo

glue

lakol

exercise book

kaye devwar

homework

devwar

number

nimero

add

azoute

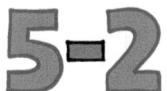

subtract

retire

multiply

miltipliye

calculate

kalkile

letter

let

alphabet

alfabet

word

mo

text

text

read

lir

chalk

lakre

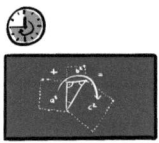

lesson

leson

register

rezis

examination

lexame

certificate

sertifika

school uniform

iniform lekol

education

ledikasion

encyclopedia

lansiklopedi

university

liniversite

microscope

mikroskop

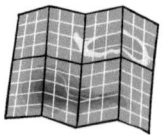

map

map

waste-paper basket

poubel

travel

vwayaz

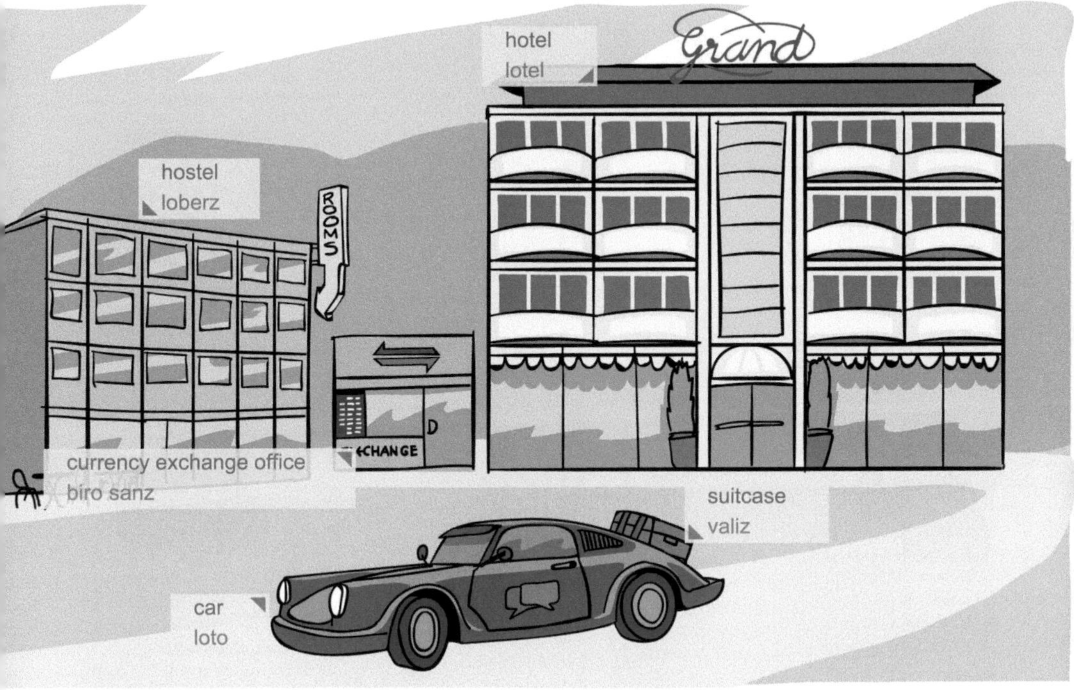

hotel
lotel
Grand
hostel
loberz
ROOMS
EXCHANGE
currency exchange office
biro sanz
suitcase
valiz
car
loto

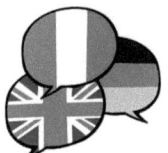

language

langaz

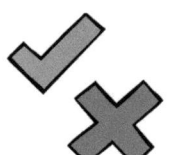

yes / no

wi / non

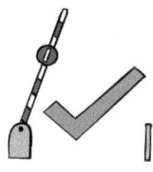

Okay

okay

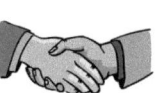

hello

Alo

translator

tradikter

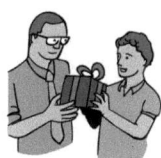

Thank you

Mersi

how much is...?

komie sa..?

I don´t get it

Mo pa pe konpran

problem

problem

Good evening!

Bonswar!

Good morning!

Bonzour!

Good night!

Bonn nwi!

goodbye

o-revwar

direction

direksion

luggage

bagaz

bag

sak

backpack

sak-a-do

guest

ot

room

pies

sleeping bag

sak kousaz

tent

latant

tourist information

lofis tourism

beach

laplaz

credit card

kart kredi

breakfast

ti-dezene

lunch

dezene

dinner

dine

Ticket

biye

elevator

lasanser

stamp

tem

border

frontier

customs

ladwann

embassy

lanbasad

visa

viza

passport

paspor

transport
transpor

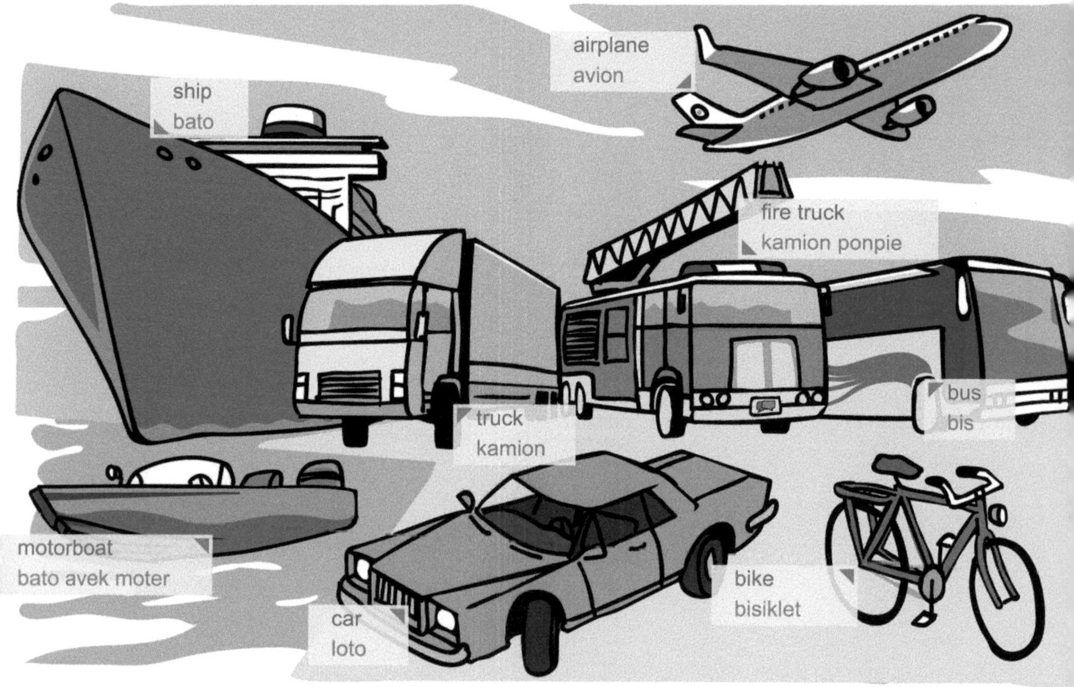
airplane
avion
ship
bato
fire truck
kamion ponpie
bus
bis
truck
kamion
motorboat
bato avek moter
bike
bisiklet
car
loto

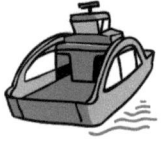

ferry

feri

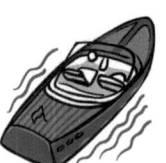

boat

bato

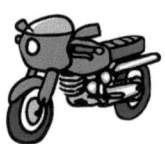

motorbike

motosiklet

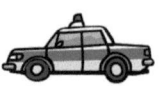

police car

loto lapolis

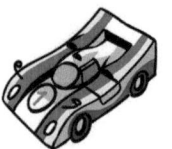

racing car

loto lekours

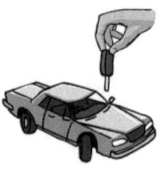

rental car

loto lokasion

car sharing

ko-vwatiraz

tow truck

kamion towing

garbage truck

kamion salte

engine

moter

fuel

lesans

fuel station

filing

traffic sign

pano indikasion

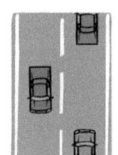

traffic

trafik

traffic jam

anbouteyaz

parking lot

parking

train station

stasion trin

tracks

ray

train

trin

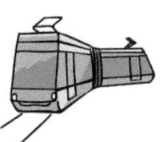

tram

tram

wagon

vagon

helicopter

elikopter

airport

aeropor

tower

towing

passenger

pasaze

container

kontener

carton

karton

cart

sario

basket

panie

take off / land

dekole / aterir

city
lavil

village

vilaz

city center

sant-vil

house

lakaz

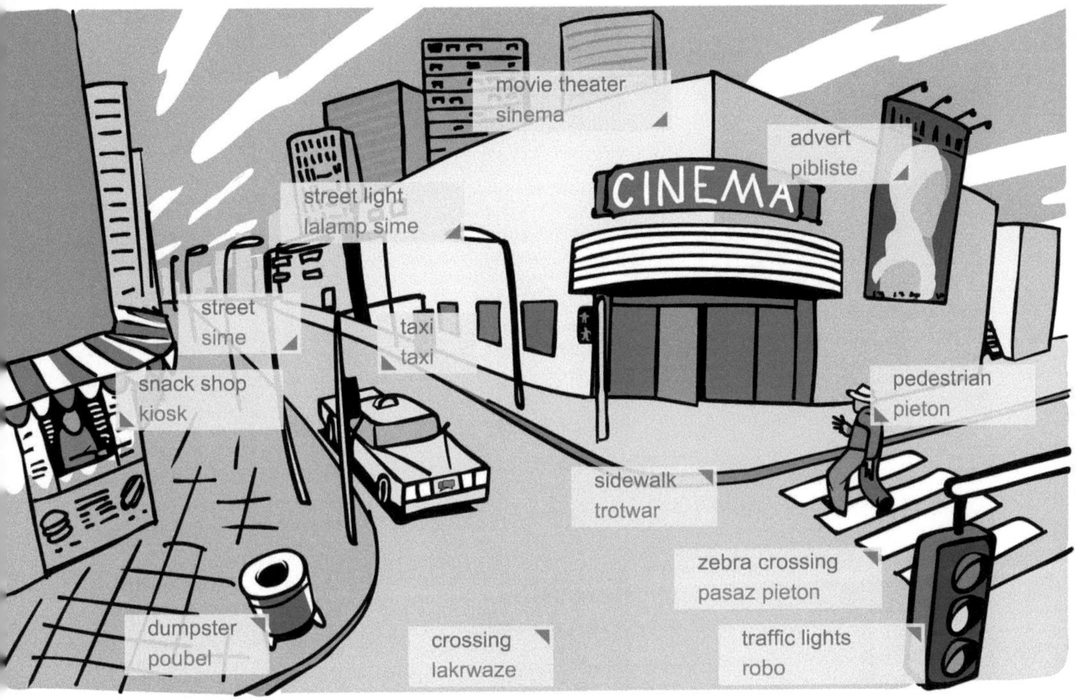

movie theater
sinema

advert
pibliste

street light
lalamp sime

street
sime

taxi
taxi

snack shop
kiosk

pedestrian
pieton

sidewalk
trotwar

zebra crossing
pasaz pieton

dumpster
poubel

crossing
lakrwaze

traffic lights
robo

hut

kabann

apartment

flat

train station

stasion trin

city hall

minisipalite

museum

mize

school

lekol

city - lavil

university

liniversite

bank

labank

hospital

lopital

hotel

lotel

pharmacy

farmasi

office

biro

book shop

libreri

shop

magazin

flower shop

fleris

supermarket

sipermarse

market

bazar

department store

gran magazin

fishmonger's shop

pwasonnri

mall

sant komersial

harbor

lepor

park
park

bench
labank

bridge
pon

stairs
leskalie

subway
metro

tunnel
tinel

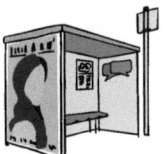

bus stop
bistop

bar
bar

restaurant
restoran

postbox
bwat-a-let

street sign
pano

parking meter
parkmet

zoo
zoo

swimming pool
pisinn

mosque
moske

farm

laferm

pollution

polision

cemetery

simitier

church

legliz

playground

lespas pou zwe

temple

tanp

landscape

peizaz

leaf
fey

signpost
pano indikasion

path
sime

meadow
preri

stone
ros

hiker
randonner

tree
pie

river
larivier

grass
lerb

flower
fler

valley

lavale

hill

kolinn

lake

lak

forest

bwa

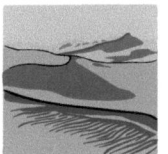

desert

dezer

volcano

volkan

castle

sato

rainbow

larkansiel

mushroom

sanpinion

palm tree

palmie

mosquito

moutik

fly

mous

ant

fourmi

bee

abey

spider

zarenie

beetle

koksinel

frog

grenouy

squirrel

ekirey

hedgehog

erison

hare

lapin

owl

ibou

bird

zwazo

swan

sign

boar

sangliye

deer

serf

moose

elan

dam

dam

wind turbine

eolienn

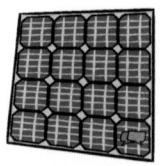

solar panel

pano soler

climate

klima

restaurant
restoran

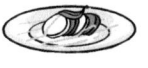

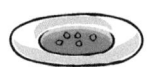

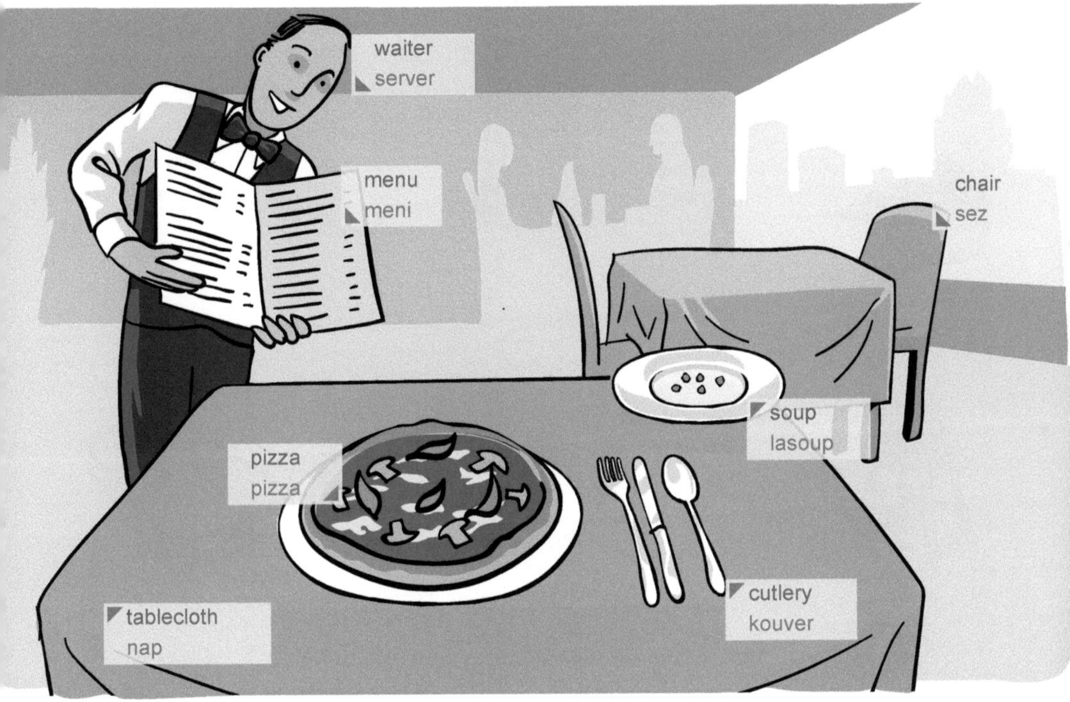
waiter
server
menu
meni
chair
sez
soup
lasoup
pizza
pizza
cutlery
kouver
tablecloth
nap

starter
lantre

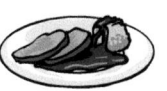

main course
pla prinsipal

dessert
deser

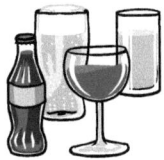

drinks
labwason

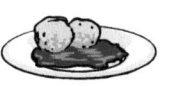

food
manze

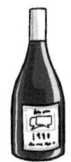

bottle
boutey

fast food
fast food

street food
take-away

teapot
teyer

sugar bowl
po disik

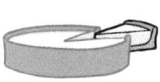

portion
porsion

espresso machine
masinn expresso

high chair
sez-ot

bill
bill

tray
plato

knife
kouto

fork
fourset

spoon
kwiyer

teaspoon
ti-kwiyer

serviette
serviet

glass
ver

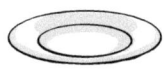

plate

lasiet

soup plate

lasiet

saucer

soukoup

sauce

lasos

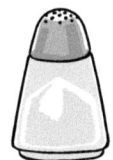

salt shaker

po disel

pepper mill

moulin dipwav

vinegar

vineg

oil

delwil

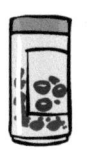

spices

zepis

ketchup

ketchup

mustard

lamoutard

mayonnaise

mayonez

supermarket
sipermarse

special offer
promosion
FOR
customer
klian
dairy products
prodwi a baz dile
fruit
frwi
shopping cart
trole

BUTCHERS

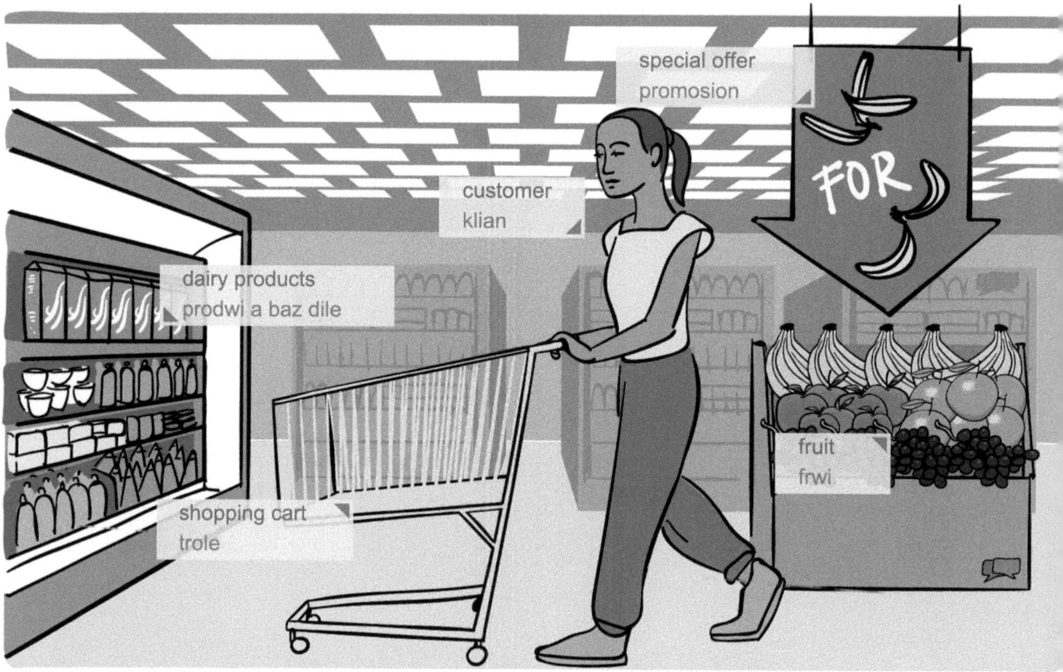

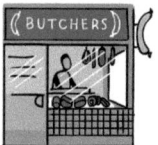

butcher's shop

bousri

BAKERY

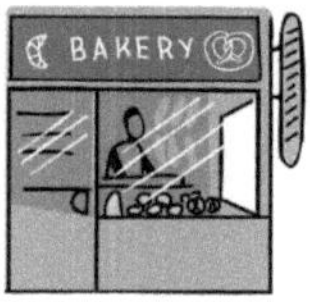

bakery

boulanzri

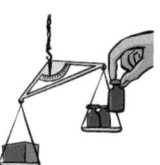

weigh

peze

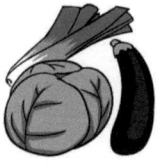

vegetables

legim

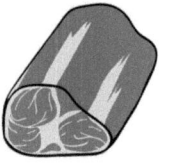

meat

laviann

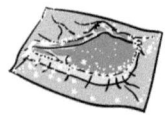

frozen food

aliman konzele

cold cuts

sarkitri

canned food

bwat konserv

detergent

lapoud masinn

candy

bonbon

household products

komision

cleaning products

deterzan

sales representative

vandez

cash register

lakes

cashier

kesie

shopping list

lalis komision

opening hours

ouvertir

wallet

portfey

credit card

kart kredi

bag

sak

plastic bag

sak plastik

supermarket - sipermarse

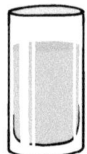

water

delo

juice

zi

milk

dile

coke

coca

wine

divin

beer

labier

alcohol

lalkol

cocoa

sokola so

tea

dite

coffee

kafe

espresso

expresso

cappuccino

cappuccino

banana

banann

apple

pom

orange

zoranz

melon

melon

lemon

sitron

carrot

karot

garlic

lay

bamboo

banbou

onion

zwayon

mushroom

sanpiyon

nuts

nwazet

noodles

minn

spaghetti

spageti

rice

diri

salad

salad

fries

chips

fried potatoes

pomdeter frir

pizza

pizza

hamburger

burger

sandwich

sandwich

escalope

eskalop

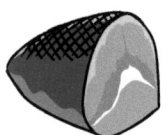

ham

zanbon

salami

salami

sausage

sosis

chicken

poul

roast

roti

fish

pwason

porridge oats
oatmeal

muesli
muesli

cornflakes
kornbif

flour
lafarinn

croissant
krwasan

bread roll
ti-dipin

bread
dipin

toast
dipin griye

cookies
biskwi

butter
diber

curd
fromaz blan

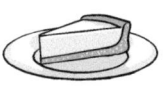

cake
gato

egg
dizef

fried egg
dizef frir

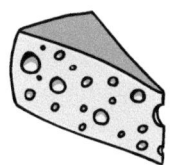

cheese
fromaz

ice cream

sorbe

sugar

disik

honey

dimiel

jelly

konfitir

nougat cream

nouga

curry

kari

farm
laferm

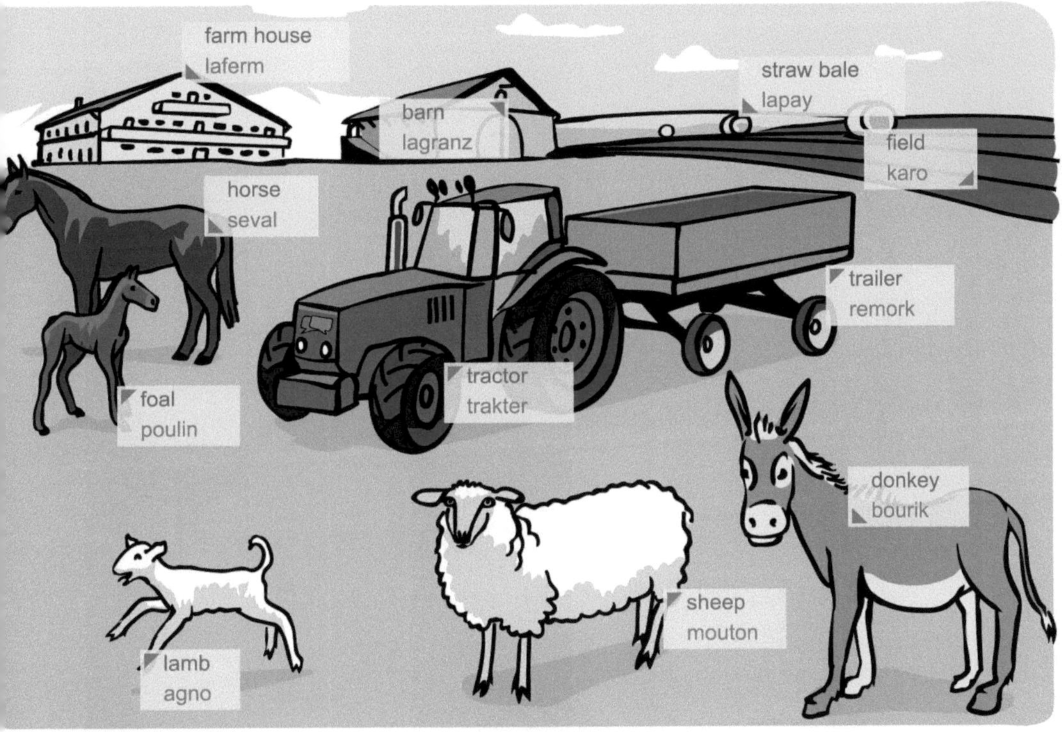
farm house
laferm
barn
lagranz
straw bale
lapay
field
karo
horse
seval
trailer
remork
tractor
trakter
foal
poulin
donkey
bourik
sheep
mouton
lamb
agno

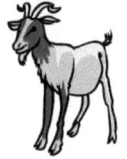

goat
kabri

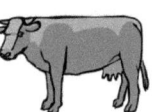

cow
vas

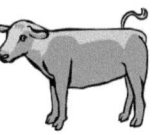

calf
vo

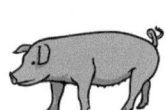

pig
koson

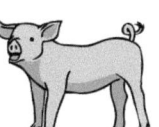

piglet
ti-koson

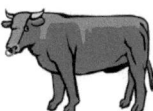

bull
toro

goose

lezwa

duck

kanar

chick

pousin

hen

poul

cockerel

kok

rat

lera

cat

sat

mouse

souri

ox

bef

dog

lisien

dog house

lakaz lisien

garden hose

tiyo

watering can

arozwar

scythe

laserp

plow

saret

sickle

fosi

hoe

pios

pitchfork

fours

axe

lars

pushcart

bouret

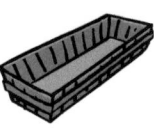

trough

kiv

milk can

bwat dile

sack

sak

fence

fencing

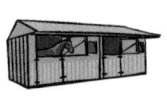

stable

letab

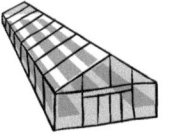

greenhouse

laser

soil

later

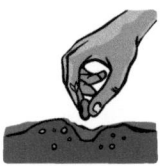

seed

lagrin

fertilizer

langre

combine harvester

masinn pou fer rekolt

harvest

rekolte

harvest

rekolt

yams

ignam

wheat

dible

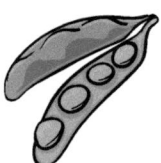

soya

soya

potato

pomdeter

corn

may

rapeseed

colza

fruit tree

zarb frwitie

manioc

maniok

grain

sereal

house
lakaz

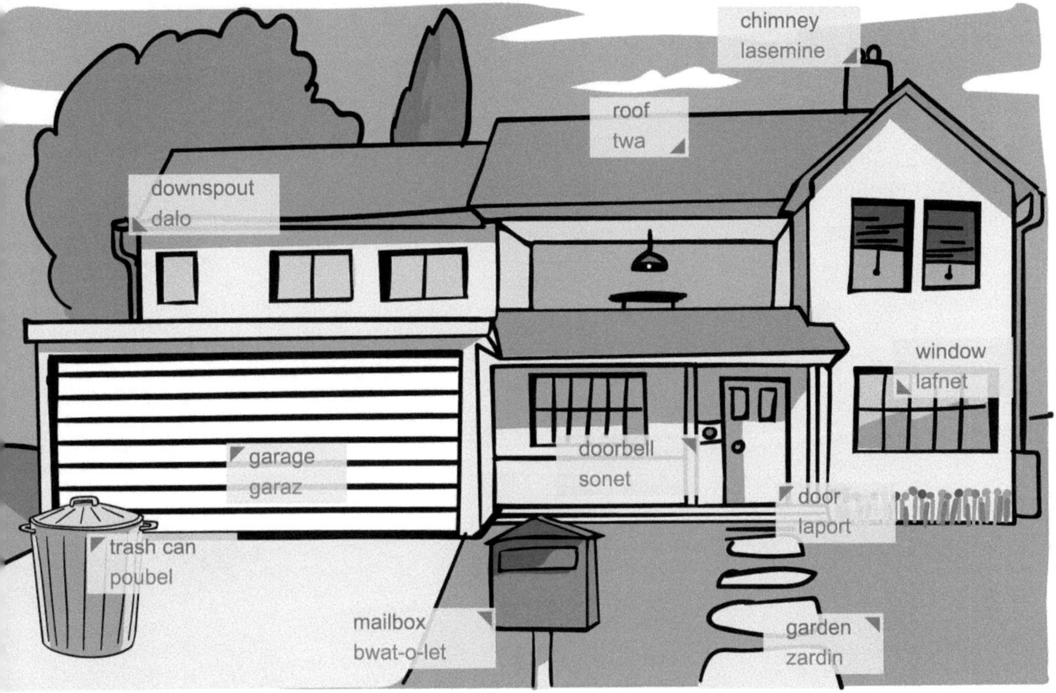
chimney
lasemine
roof
twa
downspout
dalo
window
lafnet
garage
garaz
doorbell
sonet
door
laport
trash can
poubel
mailbox
bwat-o-let
garden
zardin

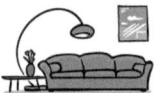

living room

salon

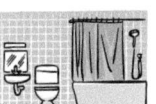

bathroom

saldebin

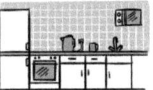

kitchen

lakwizinn

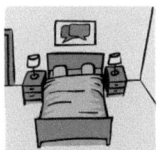

bedroom

lasam

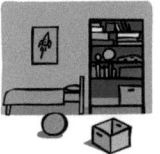

kids room

lasam zanfan

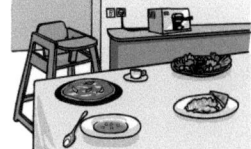

dining room

salamanze

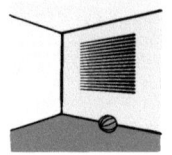

floor

sali

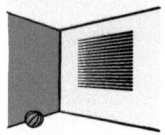

wall

miray

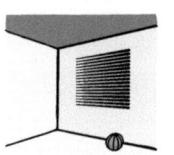

ceiling

plafon

cellar

lakav

sauna

sona

balcony

balkon

terrace

teras

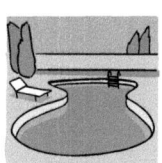

pool

pisinn

lawn mower

masinn koup gazon

sheet

dra

bedspread

kwet

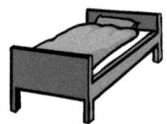

bed

lili

broom

balie

bucket

seo

switch

take lalimier

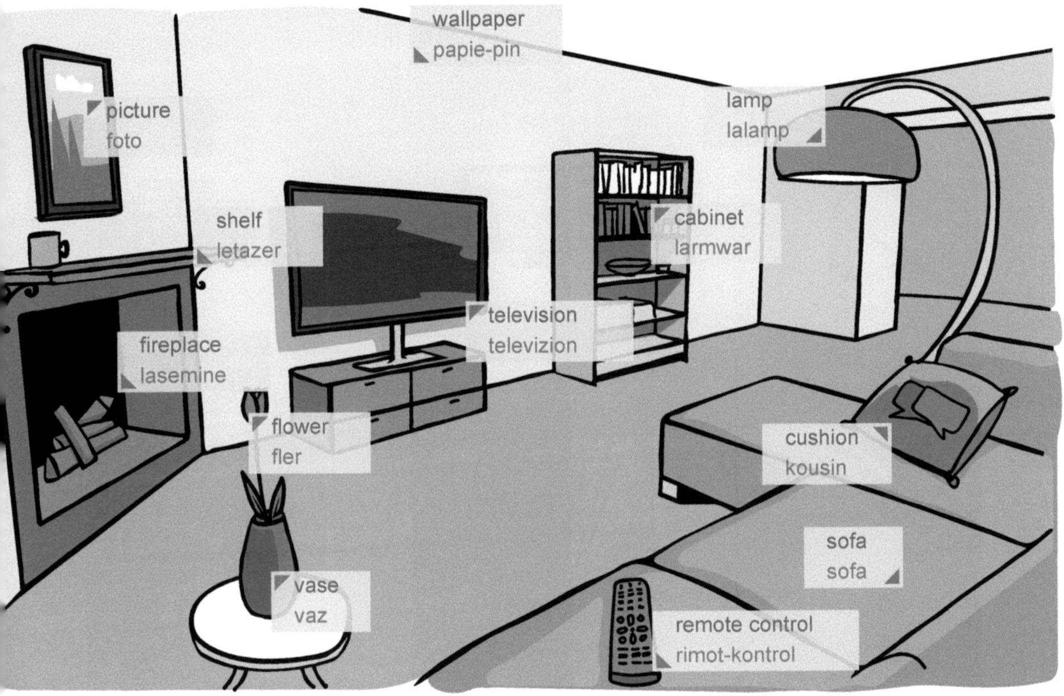

wallpaper
papie-pin

picture
foto

lamp
lalamp

shelf
letazer

cabinet
larmwar

television
televizion

fireplace
lasemine

flower
fler

cushion
kousin

vase
vaz

sofa
sofa

remote control
rimot-kontrol

carpet
tapi

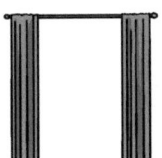

drape
rido

table
latab

chair
sez

rocking chair
rocking chair

armchair
fotey

book

liv

blanket

kouvertir

decoration

dekorasion

firewood

dibwa foye

film

fim

stereo system

hi-fi

key

lakle

newspaper

zournal

painting

lapintir

poster

poster

radio

radio

notebook

bloknot

vacuum cleaner

laspirater

cactus

kaktis

candle

labouzi

kitchen

lakwizinn

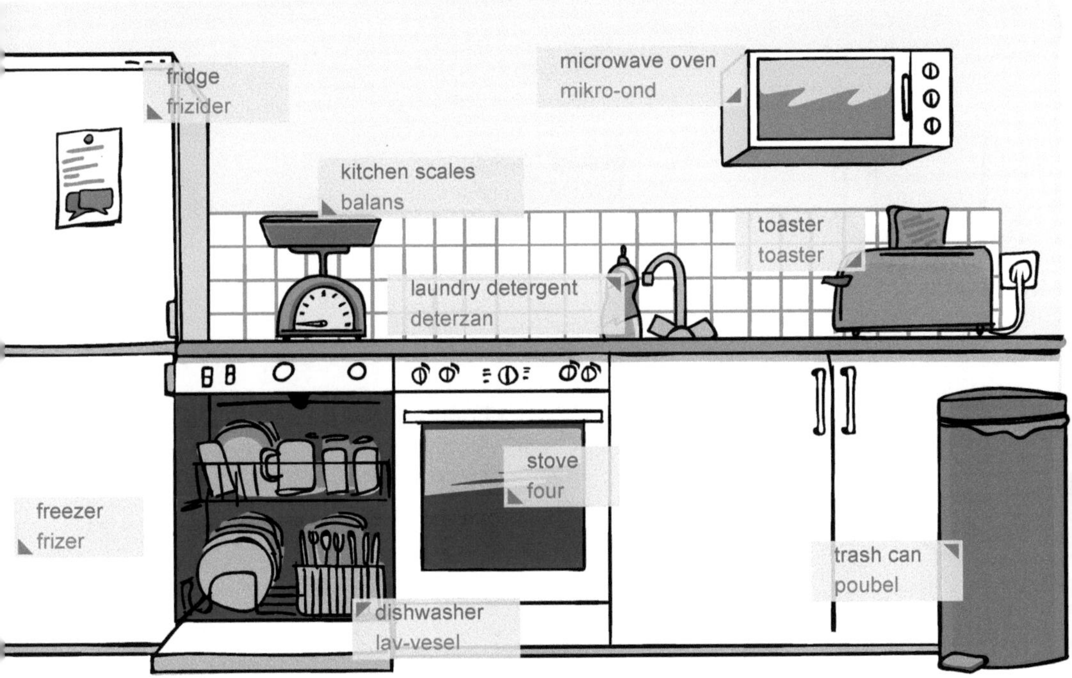
fridge
frizider
microwave oven
mikro-ond
kitchen scales
balans
toaster
toaster
laundry detergent
deterzan
stove
four
freezer
frizer
trash can
poubel
dishwasher
lav-vesel

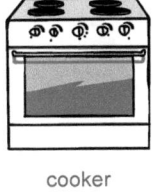

cooker

four

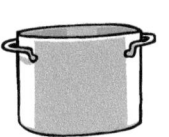

pot

kasrol

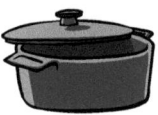

cast-iron pot

marmit

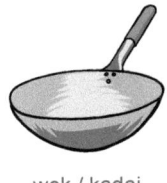

wok / kadai

wok

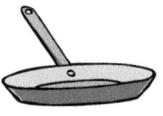

pan

pwal

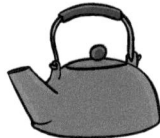

kettle

boulwar

steamer

steamer

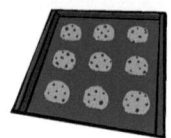

baking tray

plak kwison

crockery

vesel

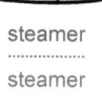

mug

goble

bowl

bol

chopsticks

baget sinwa

ladle

lous

spatula

spatil

whisk

fwet

strainer

paswar

sieve

tami

grater

larap

mortar

mortie

barbecue

griyad

fireplace

lasemine

kitchen - lakwizinn

chopping board

biyo

rolling pin

roulo

corkscrew

tirbouson

can

bwat konserv

can opener

ouvbwat

oven cloth

legan proteksion

sink

lavabo

brush

bros

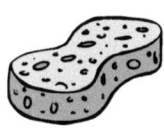

sponge

leponz

blender

blender

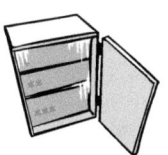

deep freezer

konzelater

baby bottle

bibron

tap

robine

bathroom
saldebin

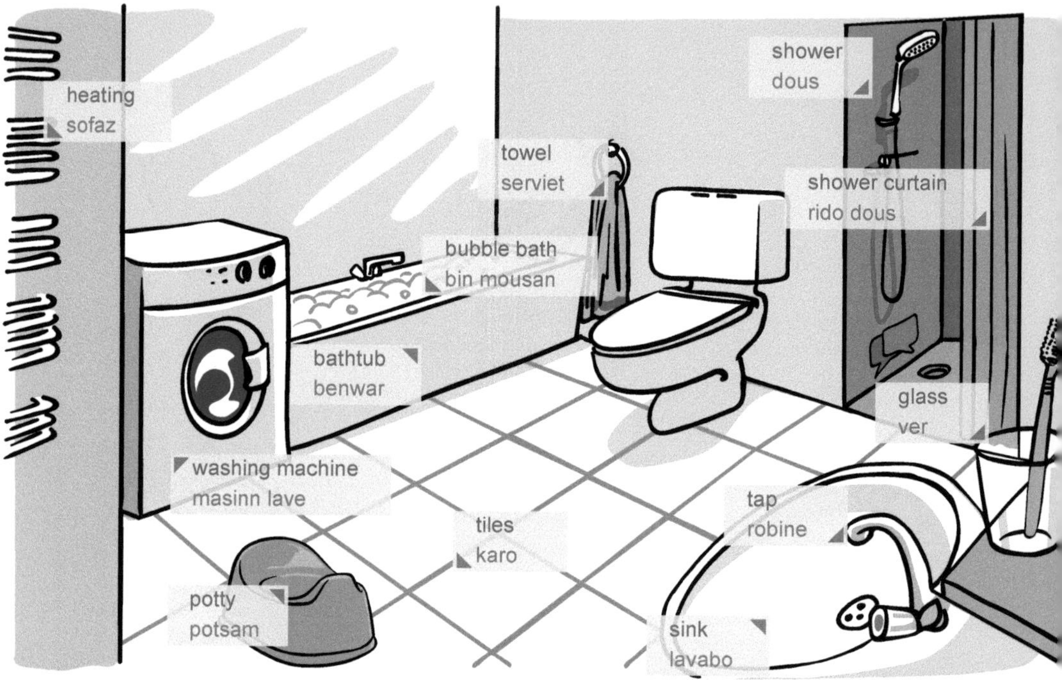

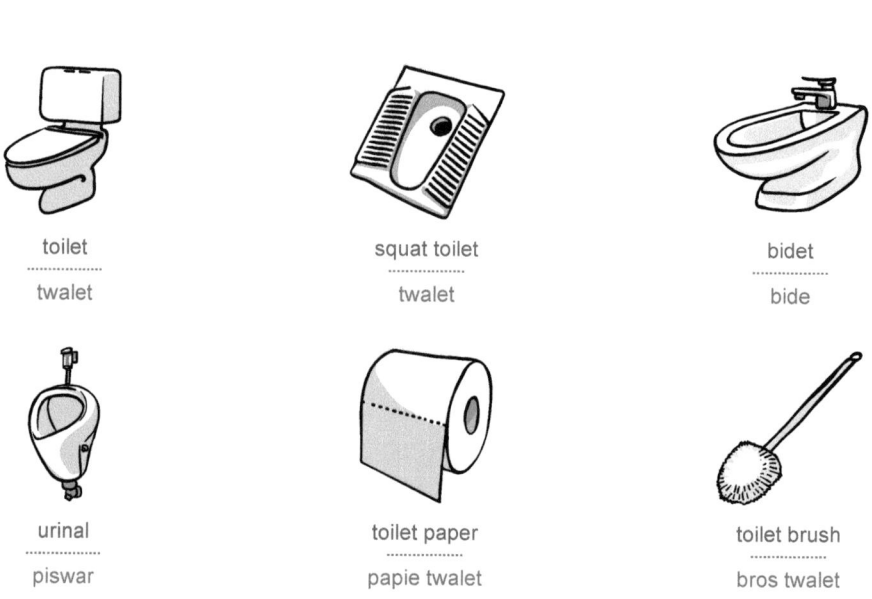

heating
sofaz
shower
dous
towel
serviet
shower curtain
rido dous
bubble bath
bin mousan
bathtub
benwar
glass
ver
washing machine
masinn lave
tap
robine
tiles
karo
potty
potsam
sink
lavabo

toilet

twalet

squat toilet

twalet

bidet

bide

urinal

piswar

toilet paper

papie twalet

toilet brush

bros twalet

toothbrush

bros ledan

toothpaste

dantifris

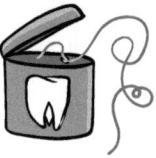

dental floss

fil danter

wash

lave

hand shower

ti-bin

douche

dous

basin

basin

back brush

bros ledo

soap

savon

shower gel

zel dous

shampoo

sanpwin

flannel

gandebin

drain

drin

creme

lakrem

deodorant

deodoran

mirror

mirwar

hand mirror

mirwar

razor

razwar

shaving foam

lamous pou raze

aftershave

apre-razaz

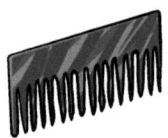

comb

pengn

brush

bros

hair-dryer

seswar

hairspray

lak

makeup

makiyaz

lipstick

dirouz

nail varnish

verni

cotton wool

cotton wool

nail scissors

tay-zong

perfume

parfin

washbag

trous twalet

stool

stoul

weighing scales

balans

bathrobe

penwar

rubber gloves

legan netwayaz

tampon

tanpon

sanitary towel

serviet izienik

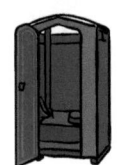

chemical toilet

twalet simik

kids room

lasam zanfan

alarm clock
revey
cuddly toy
doudou
toy car
ti loto
rattle
ose
doll's house
lakaz zouzou
present
kado

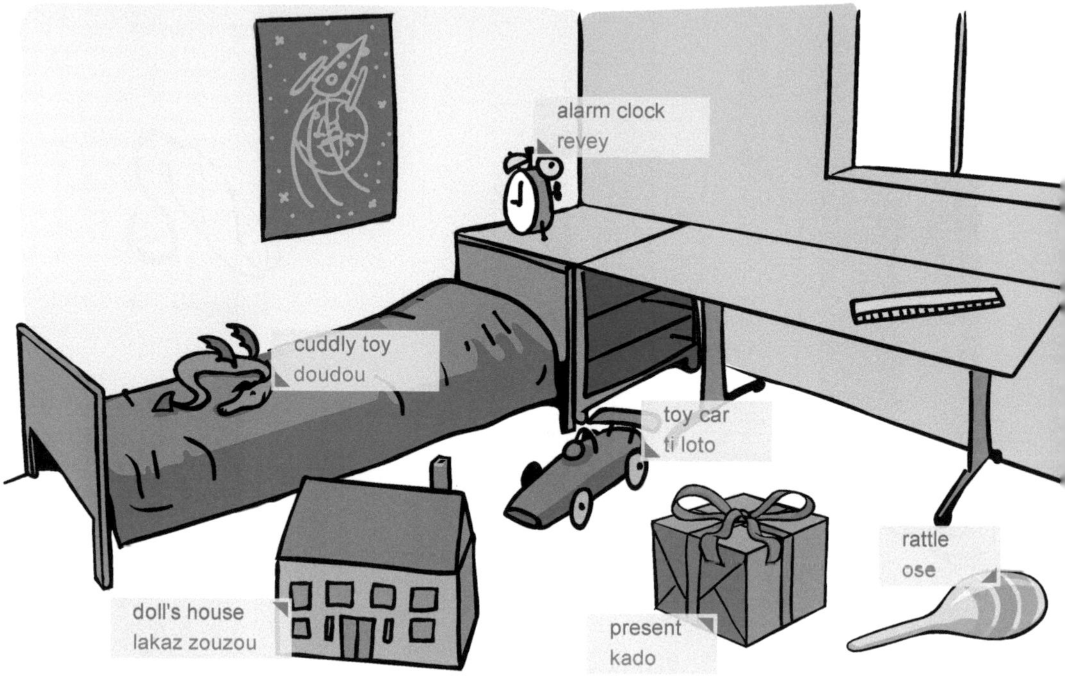

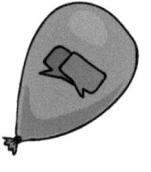

balloon

balon

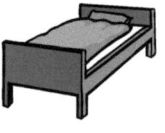

bed

lili

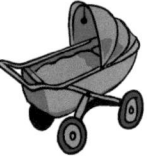

stroller

pouset

deck of cards

kart

jigsaw

puzzle

SUPER
MEGA

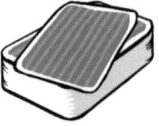

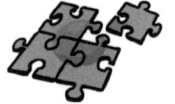

comic

tikomik

lego bricks

lego

toy blocks

lego

action figure

figirinn

romper suit

grenouyer

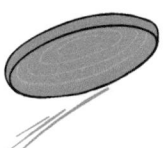

frisbee

frisbee

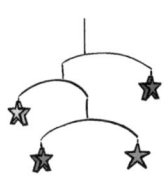

mobile

mobil

board game

zwe

dice

lede

model train set

trin zouzou

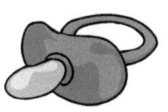

pacifier

siset

party

fet

picture book

liv ek zimaz

ball

boul

doll

poupet

play

zwe

sandpit

bak-a-sab

swing

balanswar

toys

zouzou

video game console

game

tricycle

trisik

teddy bear

nounours

wardrobe

larmwar

clothing

linz

socks

soset

stockings

leba

tights

kolan

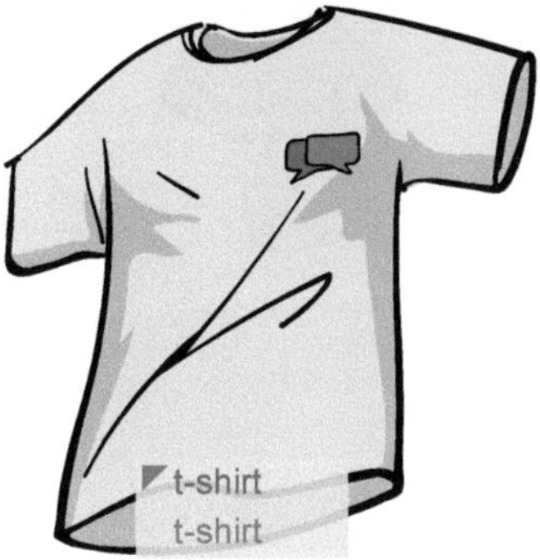

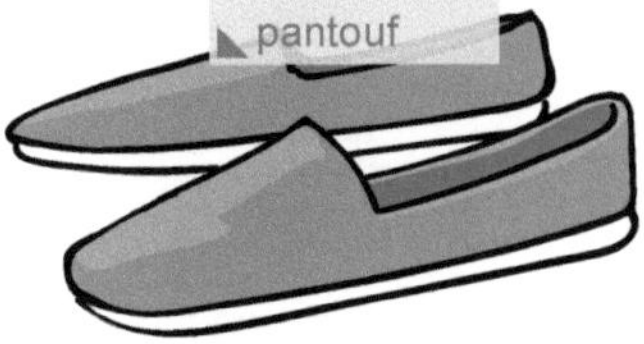

scarf
esarp

belt
sintir

umbrella
parapli

t-shirt
t-shirt

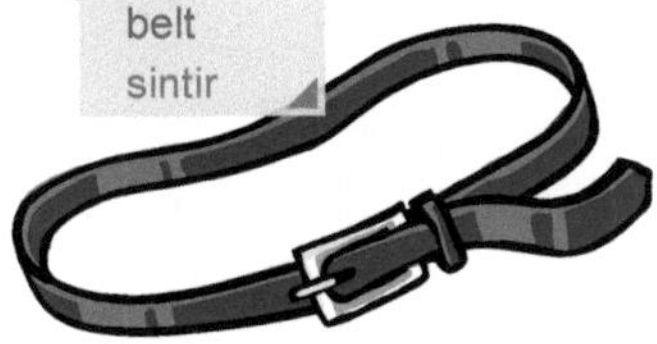

sneakers
tenis

boots
bot

slippers
pantouf

sandals
sandalet

shoes
soulie

rubber boots
bot an karotsou

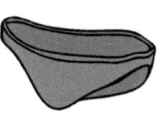

underwear
souvetman

bra
soutiengorz

undershirt
vest

clothing - linz

body

body

pants

pantalon

jeans

jeans

skirt

zip

blouse

blouz

shirt

simiz

pullover

pull-over

sweater

blouzon ek kapison

blazer

vest

jacket

jaket

coat

manto

raincoat

pardesi

costume

kostim

dress

rob

wedding dress

rob lamarye

suit

kostim

nightgown

robdesam

pajamas

pizama

sari

sari

headscarf

foular

turban

tirban

burka

bourka

kaftan

kaftan

abaya

abaya

swimsuit

mayo de bin

trunks

mayo de bin

shorts

sorti de sekour

tracksuit

linz spor

apron

tabliye

gloves

legan

button

bouton

glasses

linet

bracelet

brasle

necklace

kolie

ring

bag

earring

zanon

cap

bone

coat hanger

sint

hat

sapo

tie

kravat

zip

fermetirekler

helmet

elmet

braces

bretel

school uniform

iniform lekol

uniform

iniform

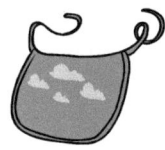

bib

bavwar

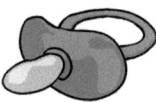

pacifier

siset

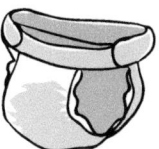

diaper

lanz

office
biro

server
server
filing cabinet
larmwar arsiv
printer
printer
paper
papie
monitor
lekran
mouse
mouse
desk
biro
folder
klaser
keyboard
klavie
waste-paper basket
poubel
computer
ordinater
chair
sez

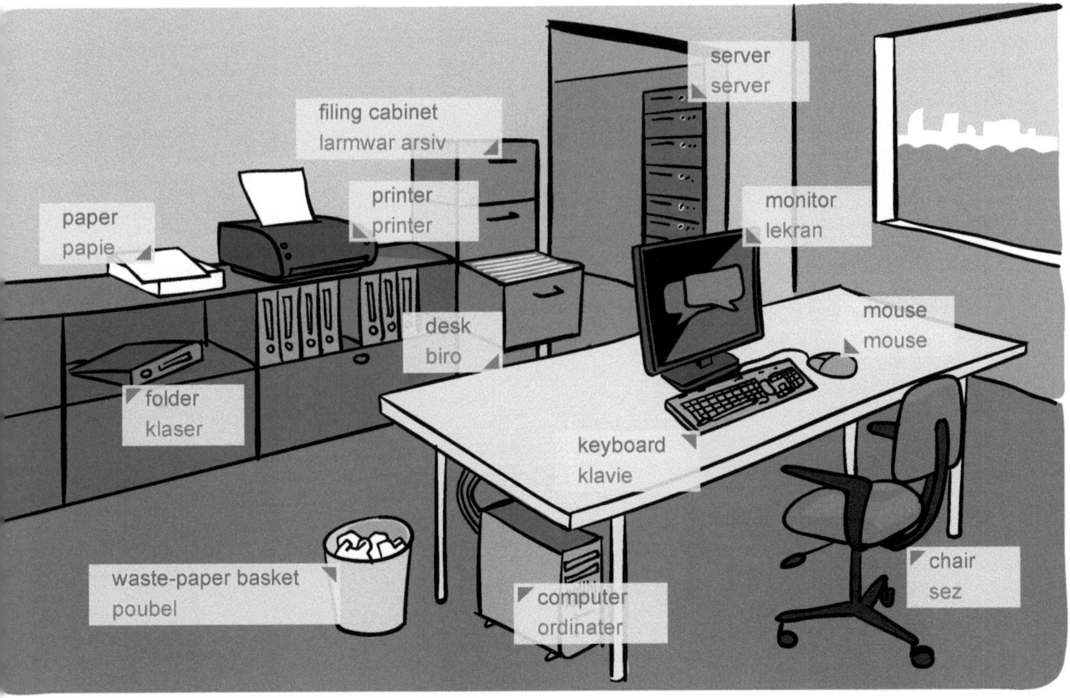

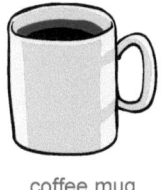

coffee mug

mug

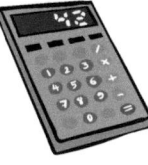

calculator

kalkilatris

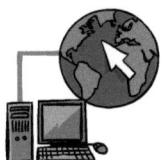

internet

internet

laptop
laptop

letter
let

message
mesaz

cell phone
portab

network
rezo

photocopier
fotokopi

software
lozisiel

telephone
telefonn

plug socket
priz

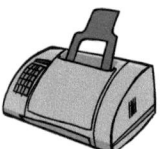

fax machine
fax

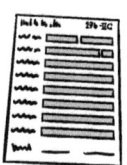

form
form

document
dokiman

buy

aste

pay

peye

trade

fer biznes

money

larzan

dollar

dolar

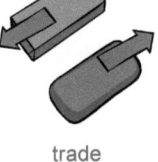 

euro

euro

yen

yen

rouble

rouble

Swiss franc

fran swis

renminbi yuan

renminbi yuan

rupee

roupi

cash point

distribiter biye

currency exchange office

biro sanz

gold

lor

silver

larzan

oil

petrol

energy

lenerzi

price

pri

contract

kontra

tax

tax

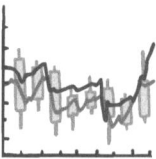

stock

aksion

work

travay

employee

anplwaye

employer

anplwayer

factory

lizinn

shop

magazin

police officer
polisie

fireman
ponpie

cook
kwizinie

doctor
dokter

pilot
pilot

gardener

zardinie

carpenter

sarpantie

seamstress

koutirier

judge

ziz

chemist

simis

actor

akter

bus driver

sofer bis

taxi driver

sofer taxi

fisherman

peser

cleaning lady

bonn

roofer

zouvriye twa lakaz

waiter

server

hunter

saser

painter

pint

baker

boulanze

electrician

elektrisien

builder

zouvriye

engineer

inzenier

butcher

bouse

plumber

plonbie

postman

fakter

soldier

solda

architect

arsitek

cashier

kesie

florist

fleris

hairdresser

kwafez

conductor

chek

mechanic

mekanisien

captain

kapitenn

dentist

dantis

scientist

siantis

rabbi

rabi

imam

imam

monk

mwann

pastor

pret

occupations - travay

tools
zouti

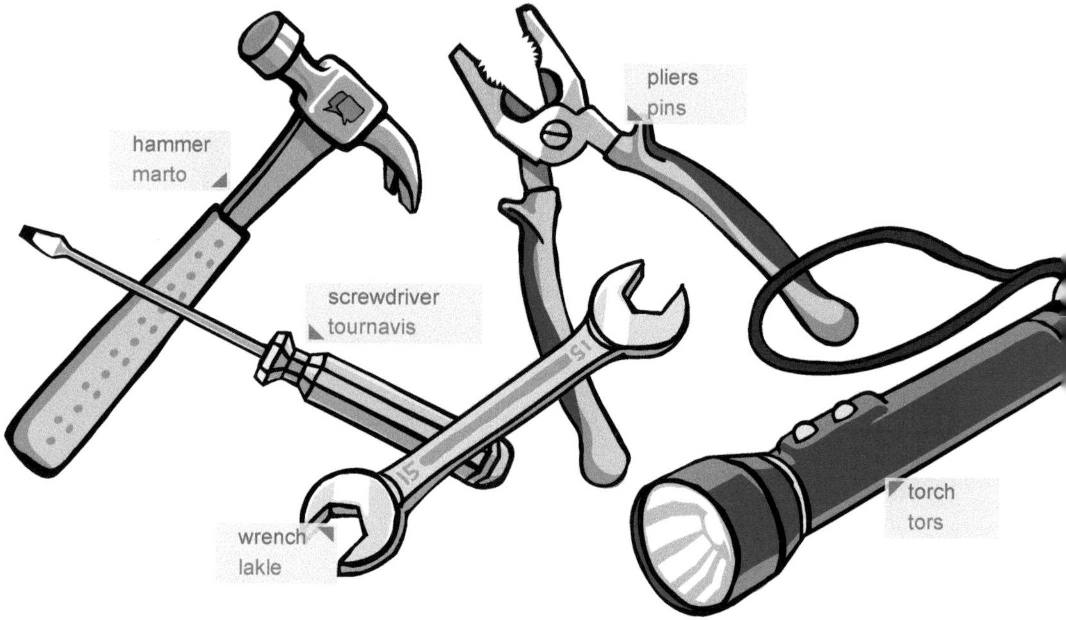

hammer
marto
pliers
pins
screwdriver
tournavis
wrench
lakle
torch
tors

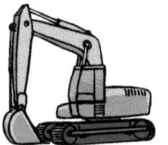

excavator

peltez

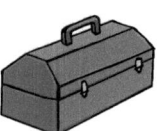

toolbox

bwat zouti

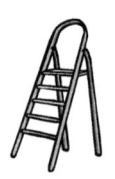

ladder

lesel

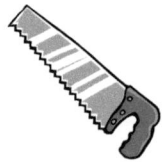

saw

lasi

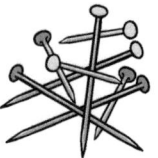

nails

koulou

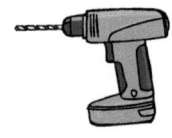

drill

persez

repair
aranze

shovel
lapel

Damn!
Ayo!

dustpan
lapel

paint can
po lapintir

screws
vis

musical instruments
instriman lamizik

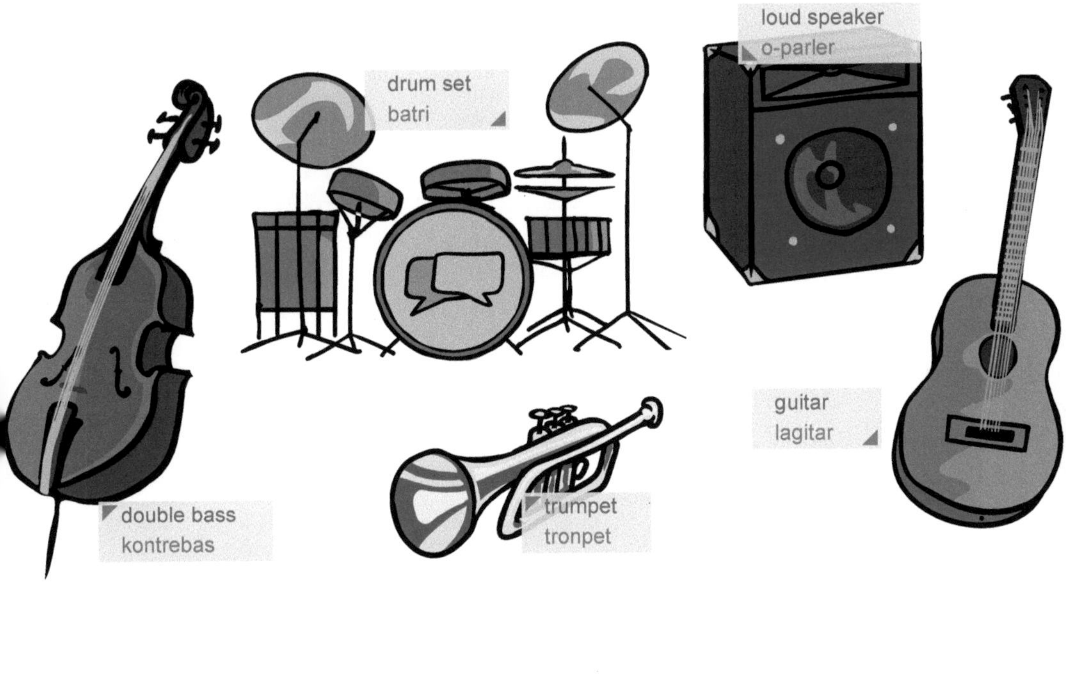

drum set
batri

loud speaker
o-parler

guitar
lagitar

double bass
kontrebas

trumpet
tronpet

piano

piano

violin

violon

bass

bas

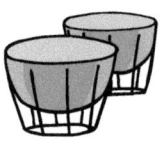

timpani

tinbal

drums

tanbour

keyboard

klavie

saxophone

saxofonn

flute

laflit

microphone

mikro

entrance
lantre

tiger
tig

cage
kaz

zebra
zeb

animal feed
manze pou zanimo

panda
panda

animals

zanimo

elephant

lelefan

kangaroo

kangourou

rhino

rinoceros

gorilla

gori

bear

lours

camel

samo

ostrich

lotris

lion

lion

monkey

zako

flamingo

flaman roz

parrot

peroke

polar bear

lours poler

penguin

pingwi

shark

rekin

peacock

pan

snake

serpan

crocodile

krokodil

zookeeper

gardien zoo

seal

fok

jaguar

zagwar

pony

poney

leopard

leopar

hippo

ipopotam

giraffe

ziraf

eagle

leg

boar

sangliye

fish

pwason

turtle

torti

walrus

mors

fox

renar

gazelle

gazel

American football
foutborl ameriken

cycling
siklism

tennis
tenis

basketball
basketball

swimming
natasion

boxing
labox

ice hockey
oke lor gazon

soccer
foutborl

badminton
badminton

athletics
atletism

handball
handball

skiing
ski

polo
polo

jump
sote

laugh
riye

hug
maye

walk
marse

sing
sante

dream
reve

pray
priye

kiss
anbrase

write	draw	show
ekrir	desine	montre
push	give	take
pouse	done	pran

have
ena

do
fer

be
ete

stand
diboute

run
galoupe

pull
rise

throw
zete

fall
tonbe

lie
alonze

wait
atann

carry
amene

sit
asize

get dressed
abiye

sleep
dormi

wake up
leve

activities - aktivite

look at

gete

cry

plore

stroke

karese

comb

pengne

talk

koze

understand

konpran

ask

dimande

listen

ekoute

drink

bwar

eat

manze

tidy up

netwaye

love

kontan

cook

kwi

drive

kondir

fly

anvole

activities - aktivite

sail

fer lavwal

calculate

kalkile

read

lir

learn

aprann

work

travay

marry

marye

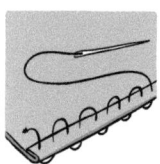

sew

koud

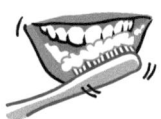

brush teeth

bros ledan

kill

touye

smoke

fime

send

avoye

family

fami

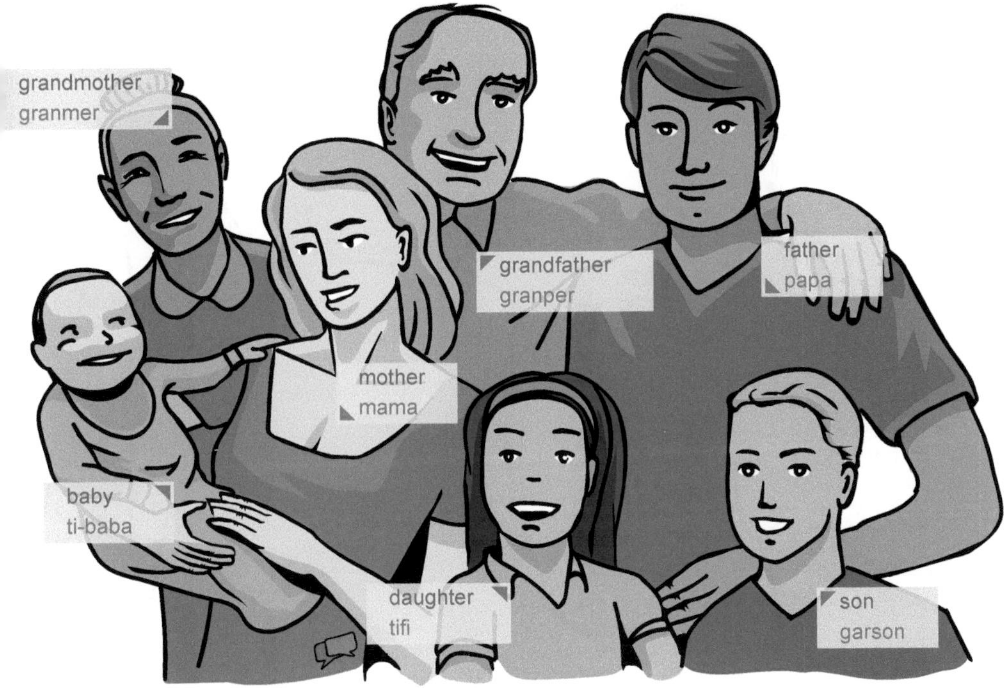
grandmother
granmer
grandfather
granper
father
papa
mother
mama
baby
ti-baba
daughter
tifi
son
garson

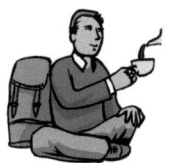

guest

ot

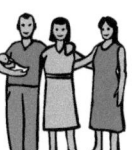

aunt

matant

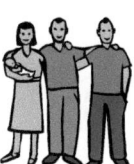

uncle

tonton

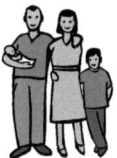

brother

frer

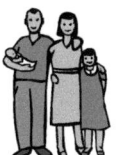

sister

ser

body
lekor

forehead
fron
eye
lizie
shoulder
zepol
finger
ledwa
face
figir
chin
manton
hand
lame
leg
lazam
breast
tete
arm
lebra

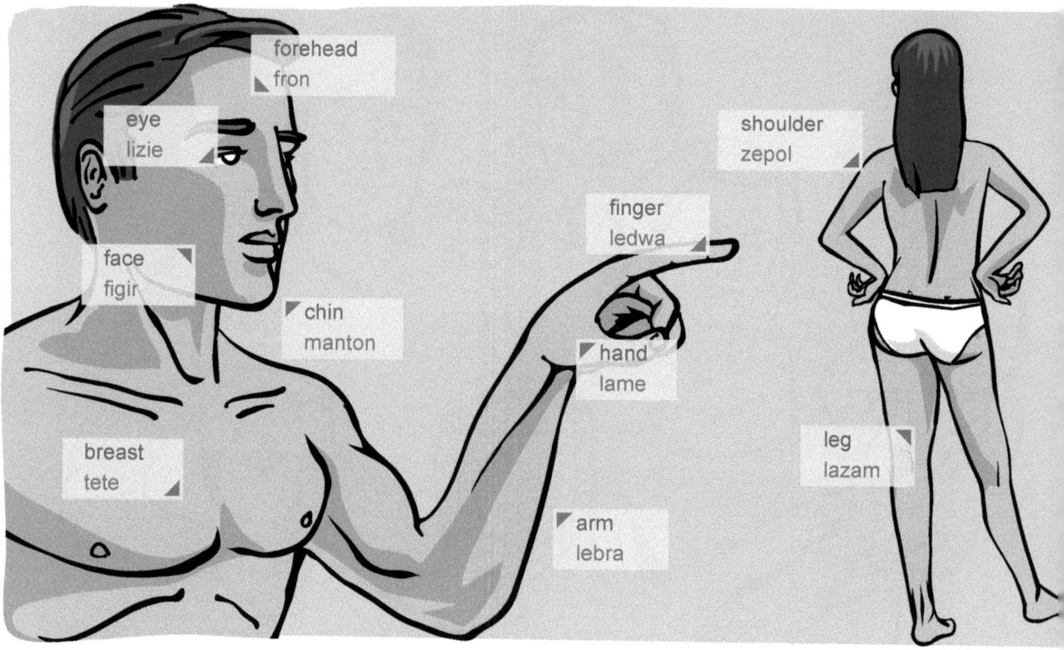

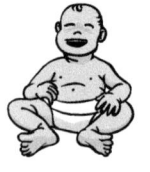

baby
ti-baba

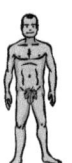

man
zom

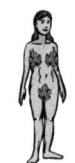

woman
fam

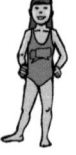

girl
tifi

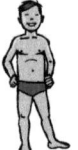

boy
ti-garson

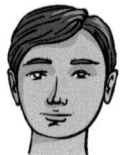

head
latet

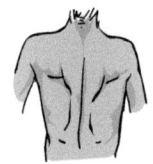

back
....
ledo

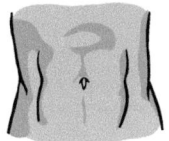

belly
....
vant

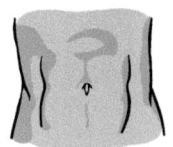

navel
....
lonbri

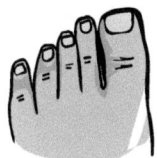

toe
....
zortey

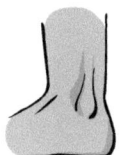

heel
....
talon

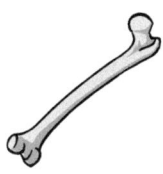

bone
....
lezo

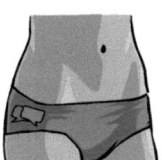

hip
....
laans

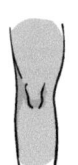

knee
....
zenou

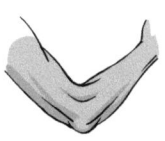

elbow
....
koud

nose
....
nene

buttocks
....
fes

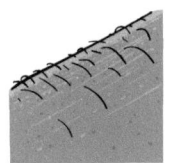

skin
....
lapo

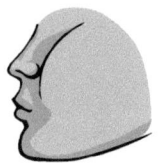

cheek
....
lazou

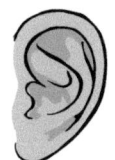

ear
....
zorey

lip
....
lalev

mouth

labous

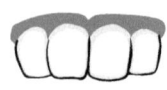

tooth

ledan

tongue

lalang

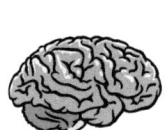

brain

servo

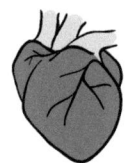

heart

leker

muscle

mix

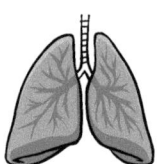

lung

poumon

liver

lefwa

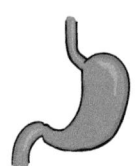

stomach

lestoma

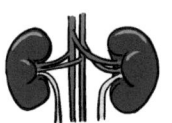

kidneys

lerin

sex

sex

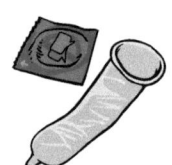

condom

kapot

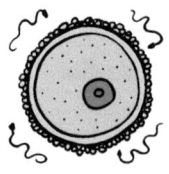

ovum

ovil

semen

sperm

pregnancy

groses

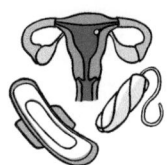

menstruation
period

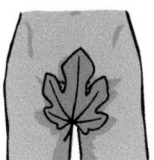

vagina
vazin

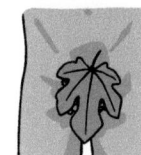

penis
penis

eyebrow
soursi

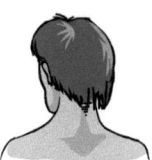

hair
seve

neck
likou

hospital
lopital

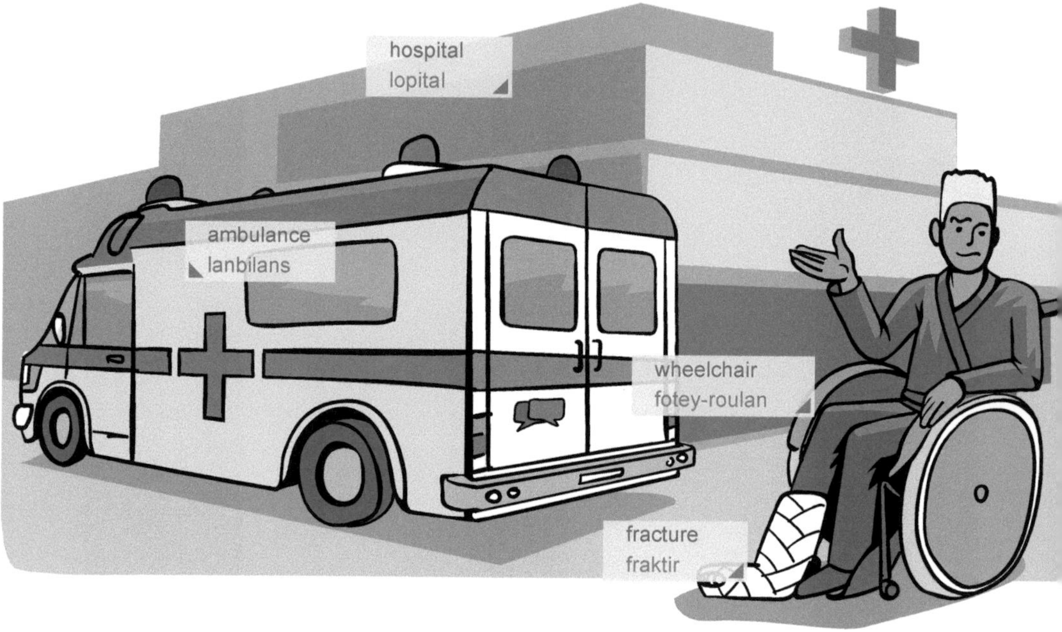

hospital
lopital
ambulance
lanbilans
wheelchair
fotey-roulan
fracture
fraktir

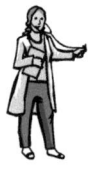

doctor

dokter

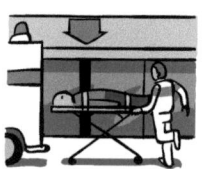

emergency room

servis irzans

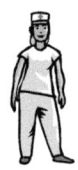

nurse

ners

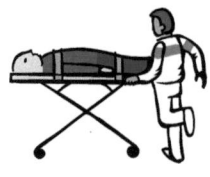

emergency

irzans

unconscious

inkonsian

pain

douler

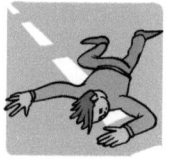

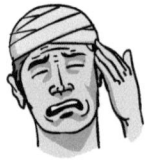

injury

blesir

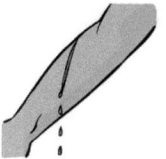

bleeding

emorazi

heart attack

kriz kardiak

stroke

atak serebral

allergy

alerzik

cough

touse

fever

lafiev

flu

lagrip

diarrhea

diare

headache

malad latet

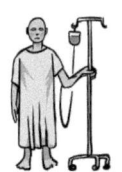

cancer

kanser

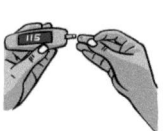

diabetes

diabet

surgeon

sirirzien

scalpel

skalpel

operation

operasion

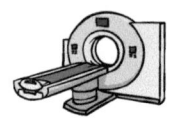

CT

CT

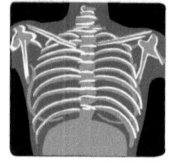

x-ray

x-ray

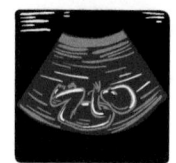

ultrasound

iltrason

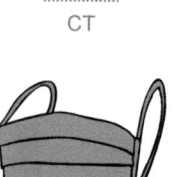

face mask

mask

disease

maladi

waiting room

sal-datant

crutch

beki

plaster

pansman

bandage

bandaz

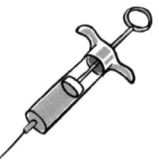

injection

inzeksion

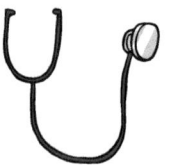

stethoscope

stetoskop

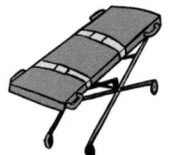

stretcher

brankar

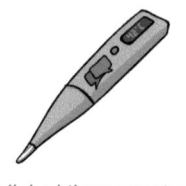

clinical thermometer

termomet

birth

nesans

overweight

sirpwa

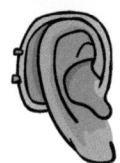

hearing aid

laparey oditif

disinfectant

dezinfektan

infection

infeksion

virus

viris

HIV / AIDS

HIV / SIDA

medicine

medsinn

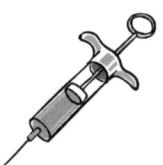

vaccination

vaksinasion

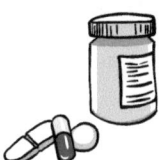

tablets

konprime

pill

pilil kontraseptif

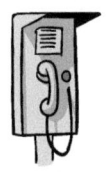

emergency call

korl irzans

blood pressure monitor

laparey tansion

ill / healthy

malad / bien

Help!	alarm	assault
o-sekour	alarm	atak

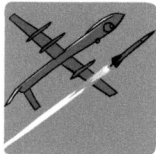

attack	danger	emergency exit
atak	danze	sorti de sekour

Fire!	fire extinguisher	accident
Dife!	laponp dife	aksidan

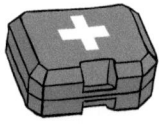

first-aid kit	SOS	police
kit first aid	SOS	lapolis

Europe

Ierop

North America

Lamerik di nor

South America

Lamerik di sid

Africa

Iafrik

Asia

Iazi

Australia

Iostrali

Atlantic

Iatlantik

Pacific

pasifik

Indian Ocean

Iosean indien

Antarctic Ocean

Iosean antartik

Arctic Ocean

Iosean artik

North pole

Pol Nor

South pole

Pol Sid

Antarctica

lantartik

earth

later

land

later

sea

lamer

island

zil

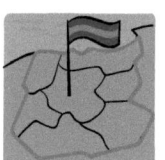

nation

nasion

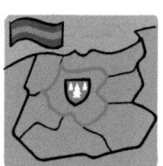

state

leta

clock face

kadran

hour hand

zegwi ler

minute hand

zegwi minit

second hand

zegwi segonn

What time is it?

ki ler la ?

day

zour

time

letan

now

aster-la

digital watch

mont dizital

minute

minit

hour

ler

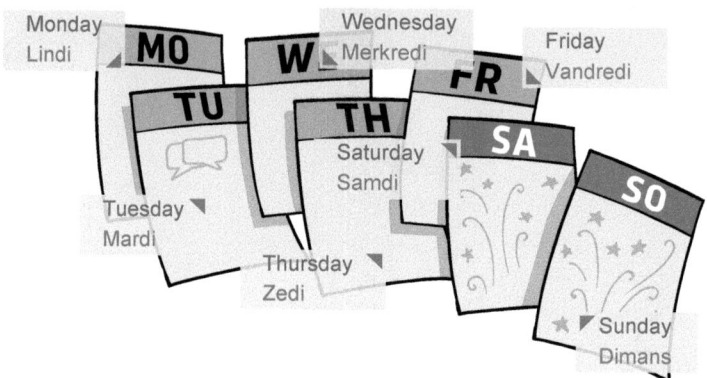

Monday
Lindi

Wednesday
Merkredi

Friday
Vandredi

Tuesday
Mardi

Saturday
Samdi

Thursday
Zedi

Sunday
Dimans

yesterday

yer

today

zordi

tomorrow

demin

morning

gramatin

noon

midi

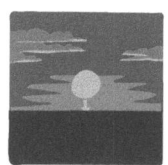

evening

aswar

workdays

zour travay

weekend

wikenn

year
lane

rain
lapli
rainbow
larkansiel
snow
lanez
wind
divan[
spring
printan
fall
otonn
summer
lete
winter
liver

4.APRIL 11°
5.APRIL 4°
6.APRIL 13°
7.APRIL 8°
8.APRIL 10°

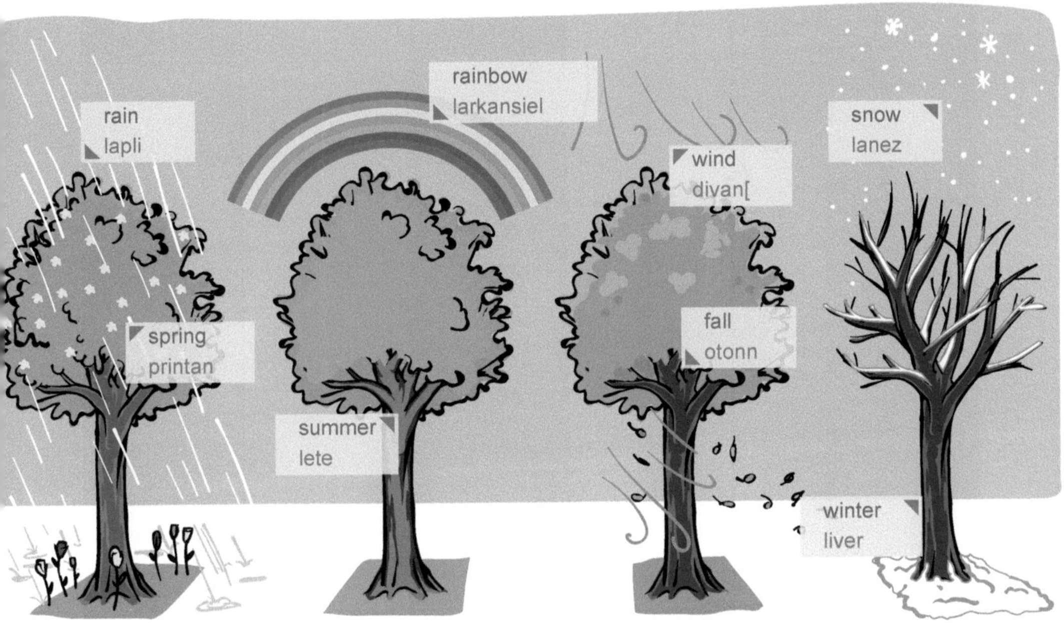

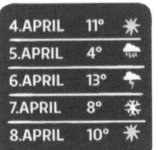

weather forecast

meteo

F C
120 40
90 30
60 20
30 10
0 0
-30 -10
-20

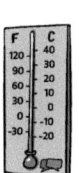

thermometer

termomet

sunshine

lalimier soley

cloud

niaz

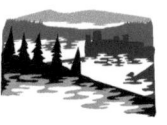

fog

brouyar

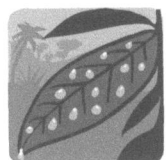

humidity

limidite

lightning

lafoud

thunder

toner

storm

tanpet

hail

lagrel

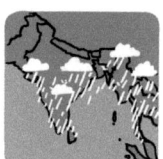

monsoon

mouson

flood

inondasion

ice

laglas

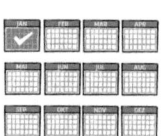

January

Zanvie

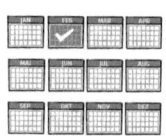

February

Fevriye

March

Mars

April

Avril

May

Me

June

Zien

July

Zilie

August

Out

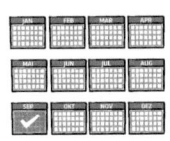

September
....
Septam

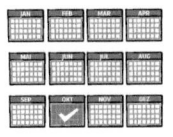

October
....
Oktob

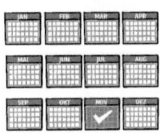

November
....
Novam

December
....
Desam

shapes
form

circle
....
ron

square
....
kare

rectangle
....
rektang

triangle
....
triang

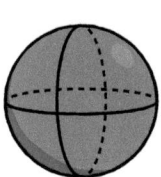

sphere
....
sfer

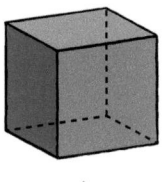

cube
....
kib

colors

bann kouler

white
blan

yellow
zonn

orange
oranz

pink
roz

red
rouz

purple
mov

blue
ble

green
ver

brown
maron

gray
gri

black
nwar

a lot / a little

boukou / enn tigit

angry / calm

ankoler / kalm

beautiful / ugly

zoli / vilin

beginning / end

koumansman / lafin

big / small

gro / tipti

bright / dark

kler / obskirite

brother / sister

frer / ser

clean / dirty

prop / sal

complete / incomplete

konple / inkonple

day / night

lizour / lanwit

dead / alive

vivan / mor

wide / narrow

larz / sere

edible / inedible

komestib / inkomestib

evil / kind

move / bon

excited / bored

exsite / agase

fat / thin

gra / mins

first / last

premie / dernie

friend / enemy

kamwad / lennmi

full / empty

ranpli / vid

hard / soft

dir / mou

heavy / light

lour / leze

hunger / thirst

fin / swaf

ill / healthy

malad / bien

illegal / legal

ilegal / legal

intelligent / stupid

intelizan / kouyon

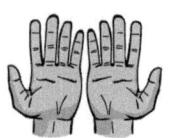

left / right

gos / drwat

near / far

pre / lwin

opposites - opozision

new / used

nouvo / ize

nothing / something

nanye / kiksoz

old / young

vie / zenn

on / off

demare / arete

open / closed

ouver / ferme

quiet / loud

trankil / for

rich / poor

ris / pov

right / wrong

bon / move

rough / smooth

brit / lis

sad / happy

tris / zwaye

short / long

kourt / long

slow / fast

lan / rapid

wet / dry

tranpe / sek

warm / cool

so / fre

war / peace

lager / lape

opposites - opozision

0

zero

zero

1

one

enn

2

two

de

3

three

trwa

4

four

kat

5

five

sink

6

six

sis

7

seven

set

8

eight

wit

9

nine

nef

10

ten

distribiter biye

11

eleven

onz

12

twelve

douz

13

thirteen

trez

14

fourteen

katorz

15

fifteen

kinz

16

sixteen

sez

17

seventeen

diset

18

eighteen

dizwit

19

nineteen

diznef

20

twenty

vin

100

hundred

san

1.000

thousand

mil

1.000.000

million

milyon

languages
bann langaz

English

Angle

American English

Angle Lamerik

Chinese Mandarin

Mandarin Sinwa

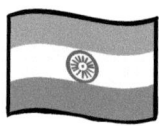

Hindi

Hindi

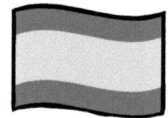

Spanish

espagnol

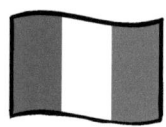

French

Franse

Arabic

Arab

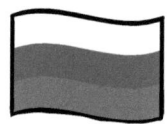

Russian

Ris

Portuguese

Portige

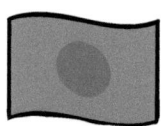

Bengali

Bengali

German

Alman

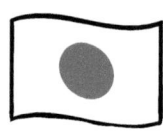

Japanese

Zapone

I

mo

you

to

he / she / it

li

we

nou

you

ou

they

zot

who?

kisana?

what?

kiete?

how?

kouma?

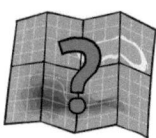

where?

kotsa?

when?

kan?

name

nom

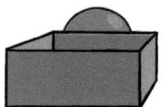

behind

deryer

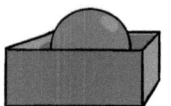

in

dan

in front of

devan

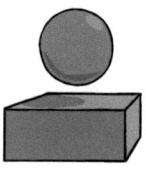

over

lor

on

lor

under

anba

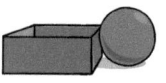

beside

akote

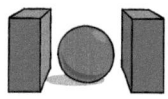

between

ant

place

plas